Inspiring Words From the Heart Adult Coloring Book

By Peaceful Mind Adult Coloring Books

Copyright © 2015

Love

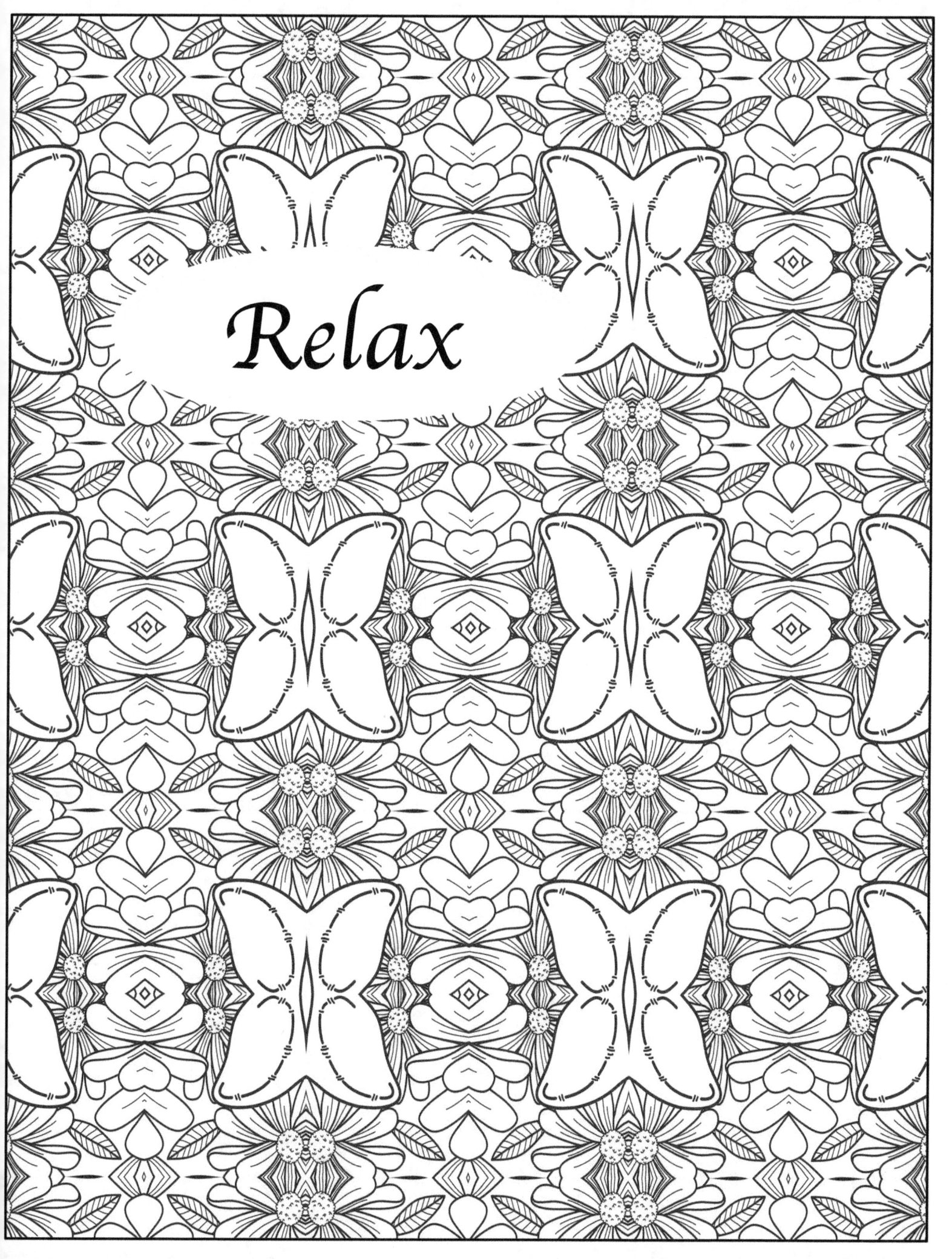

Relax

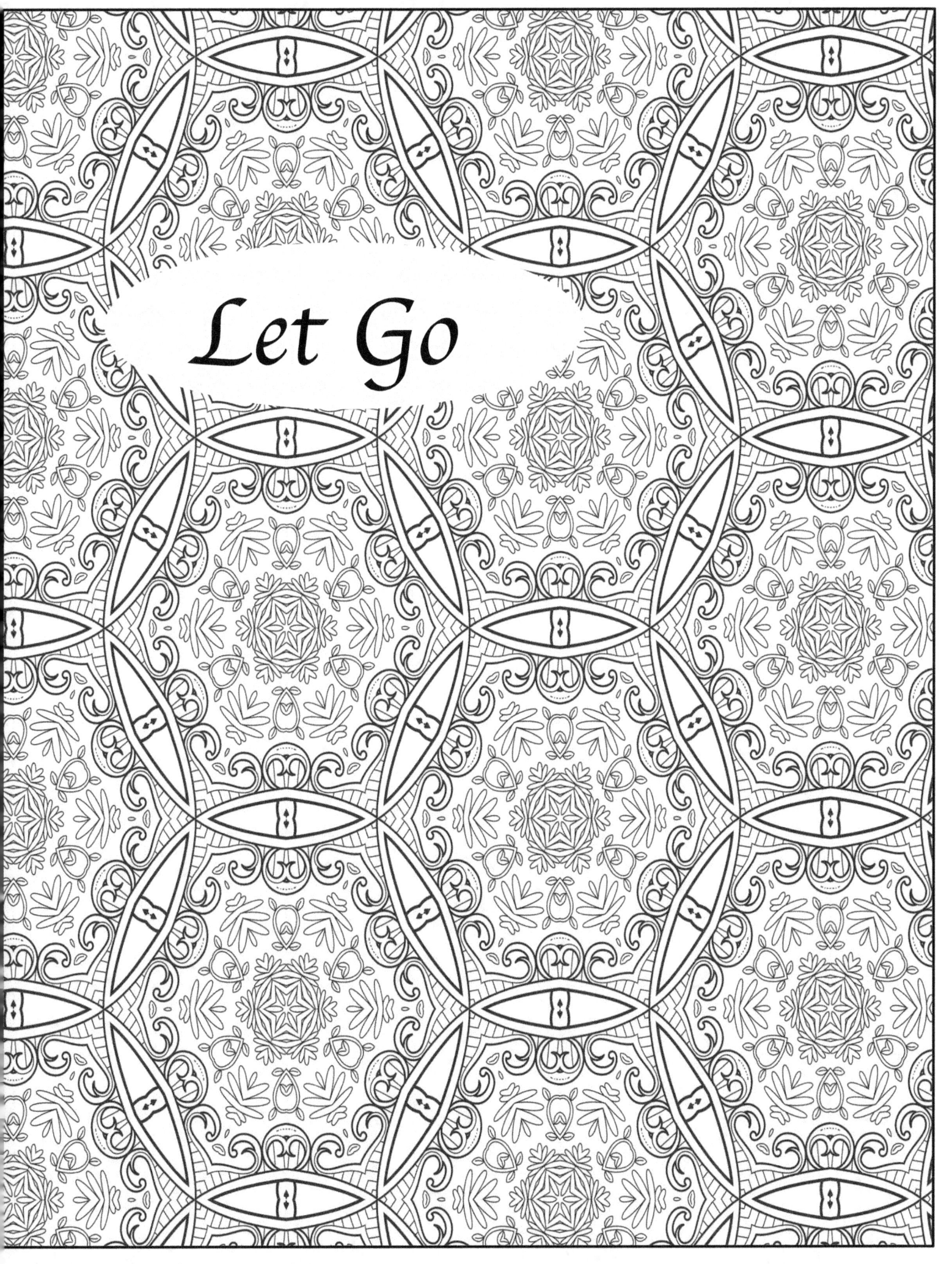

Let Go

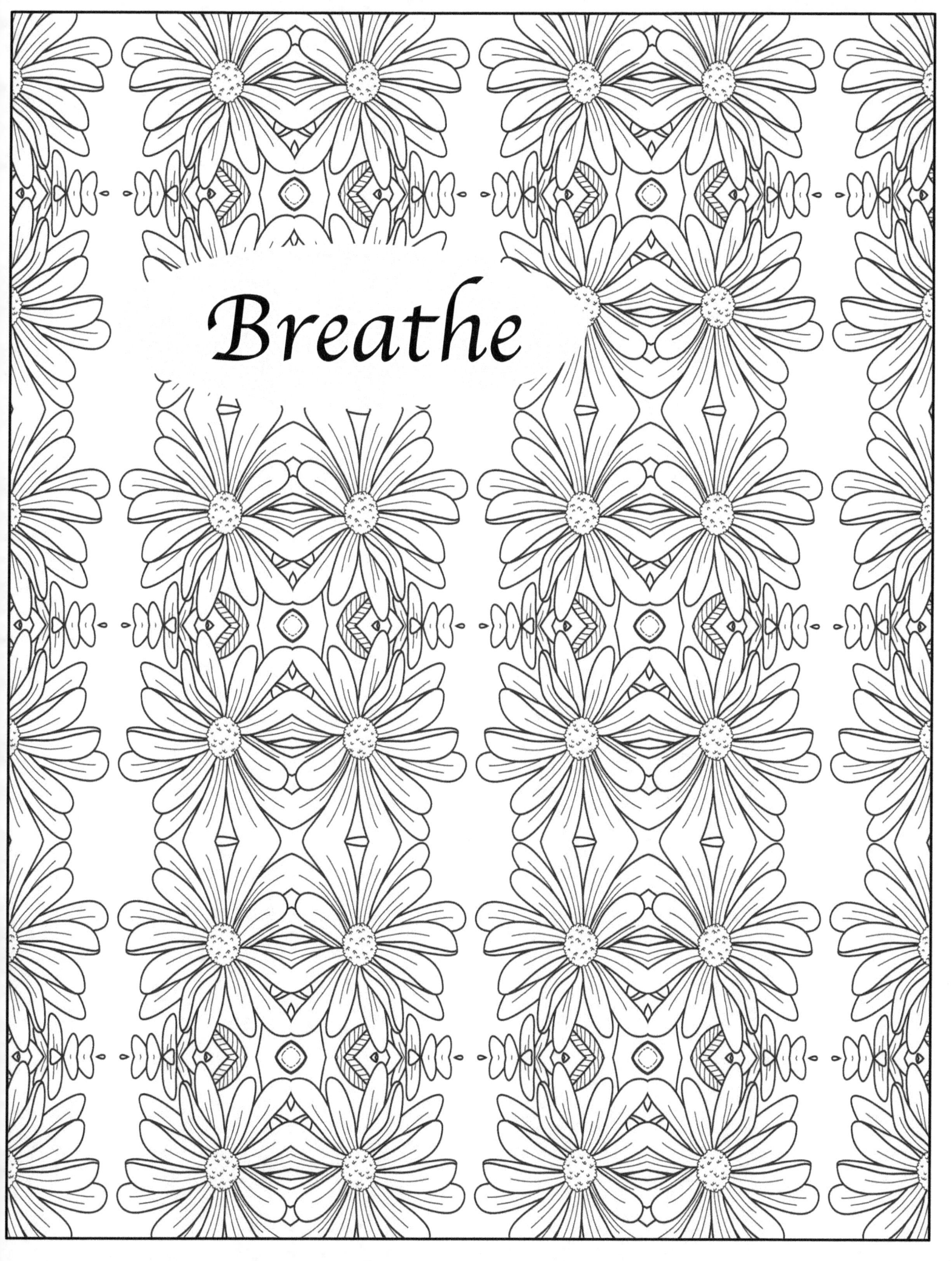

Breathe

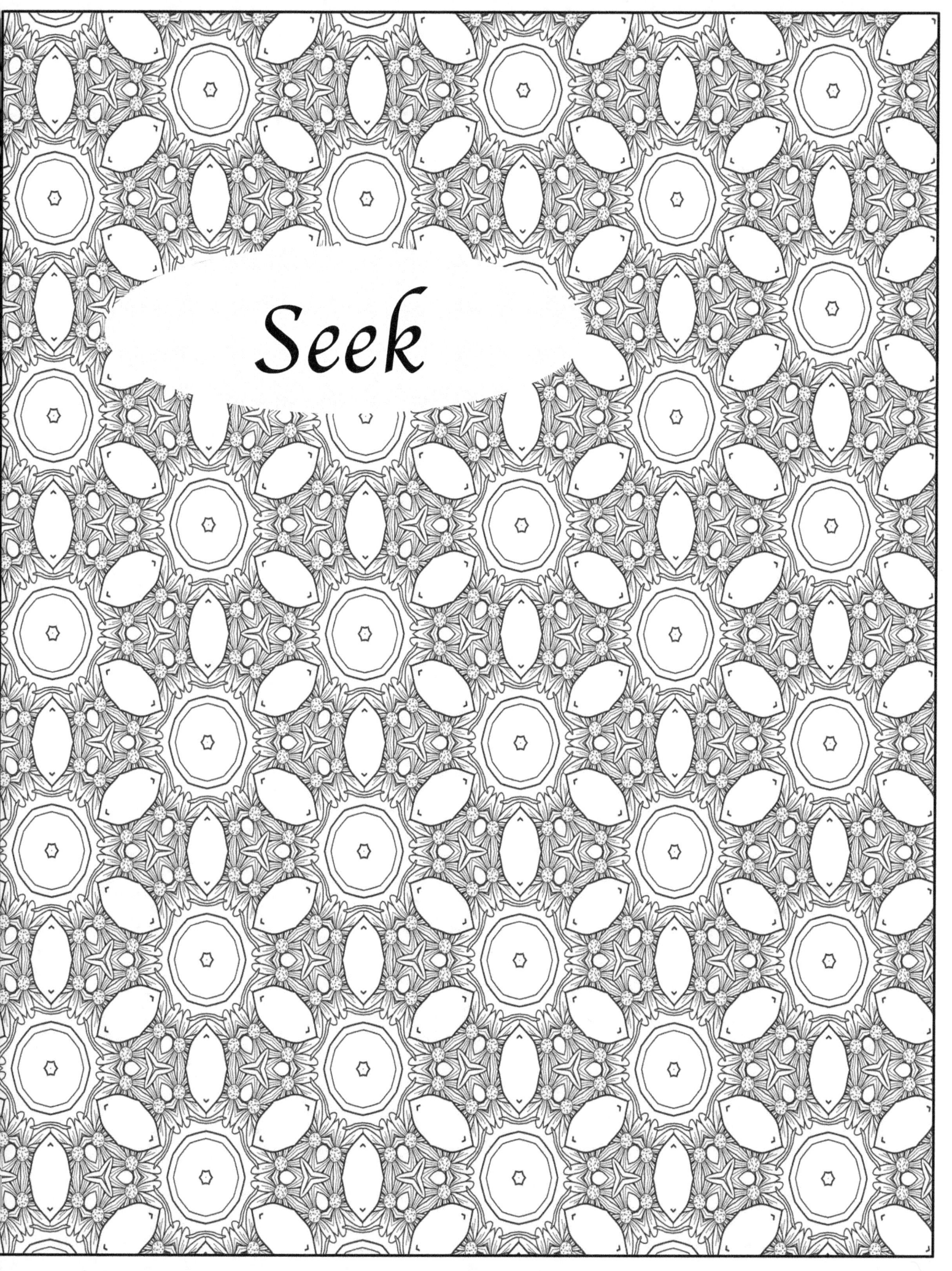

Seek

Hug

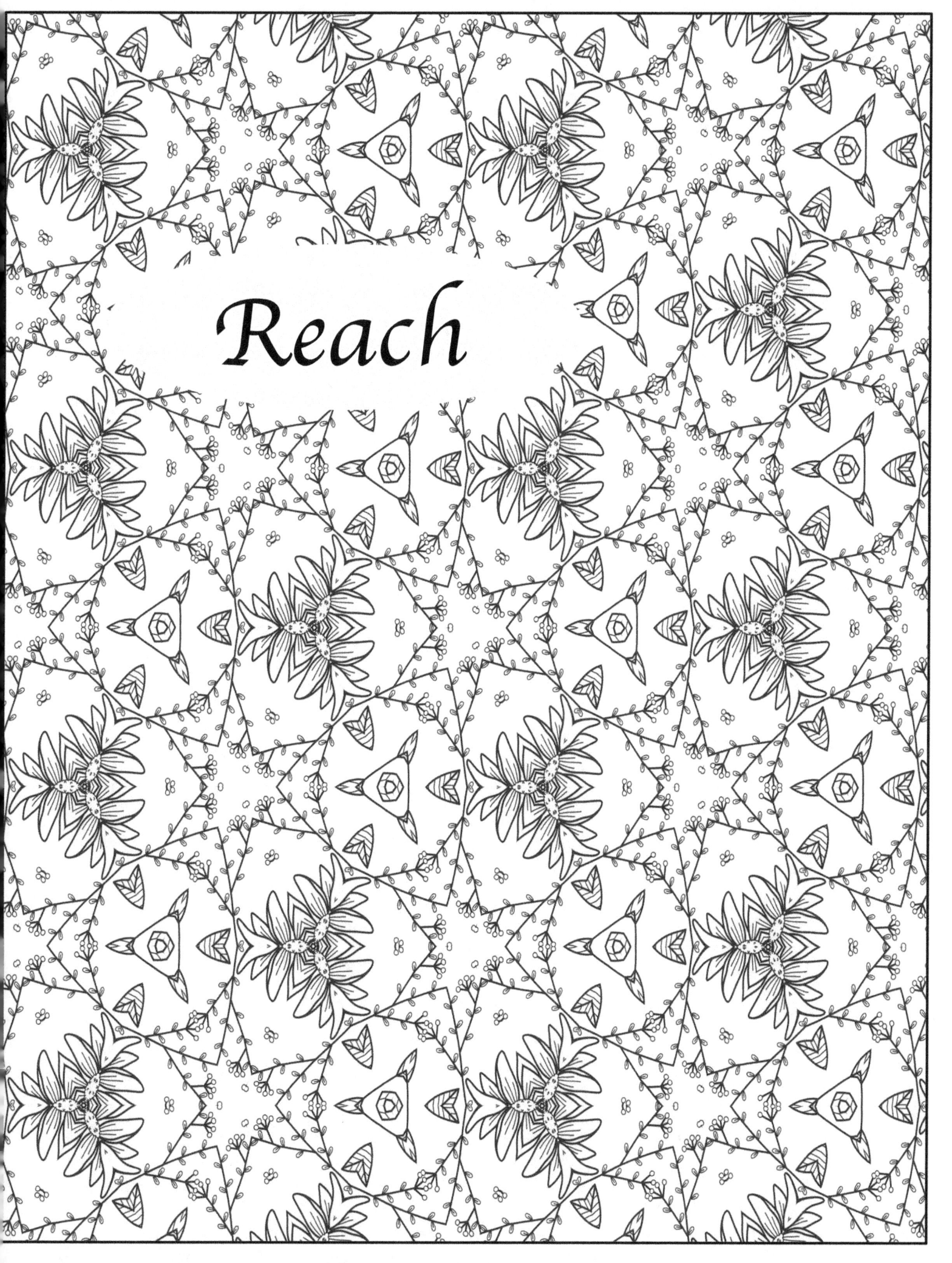

Reach

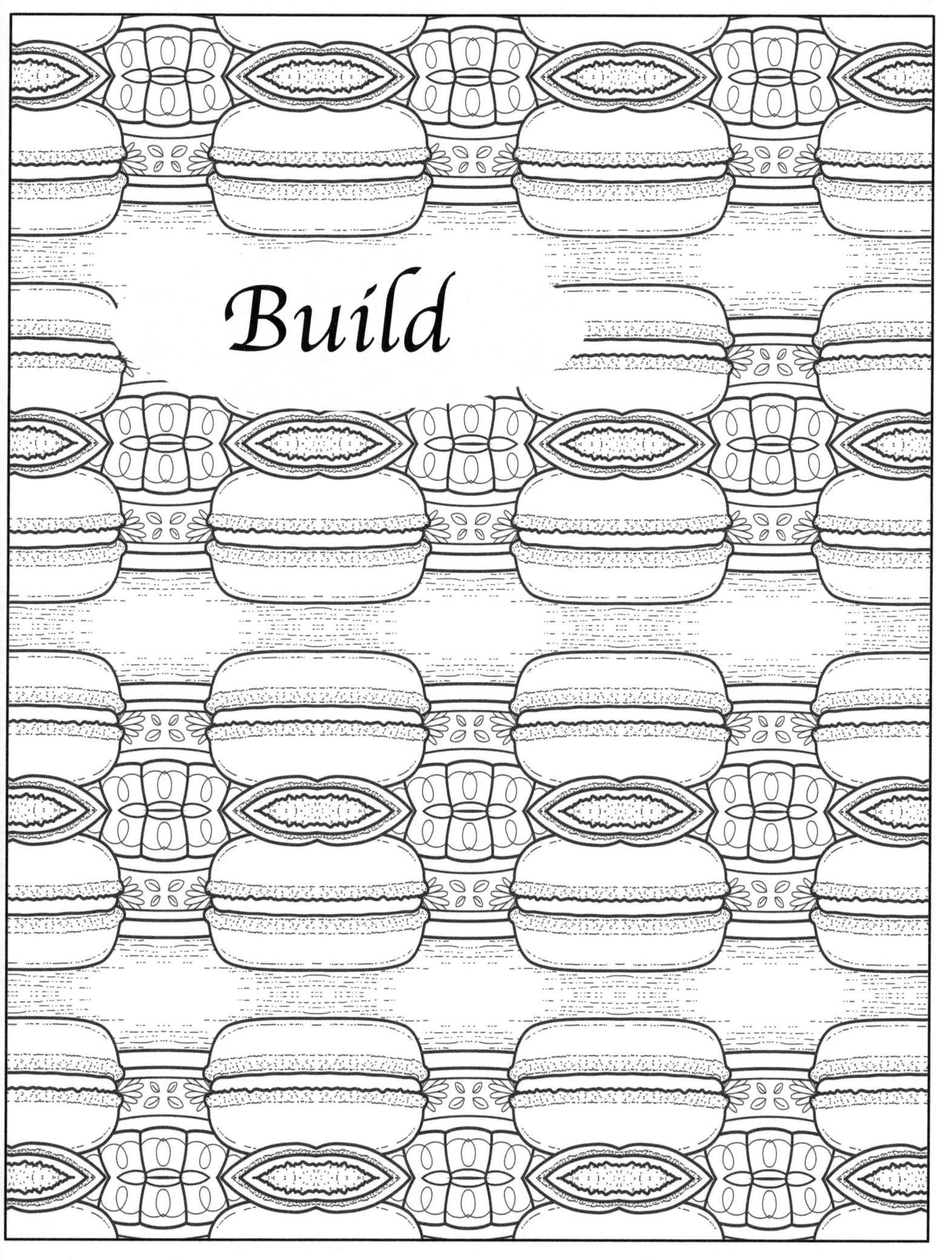

Build

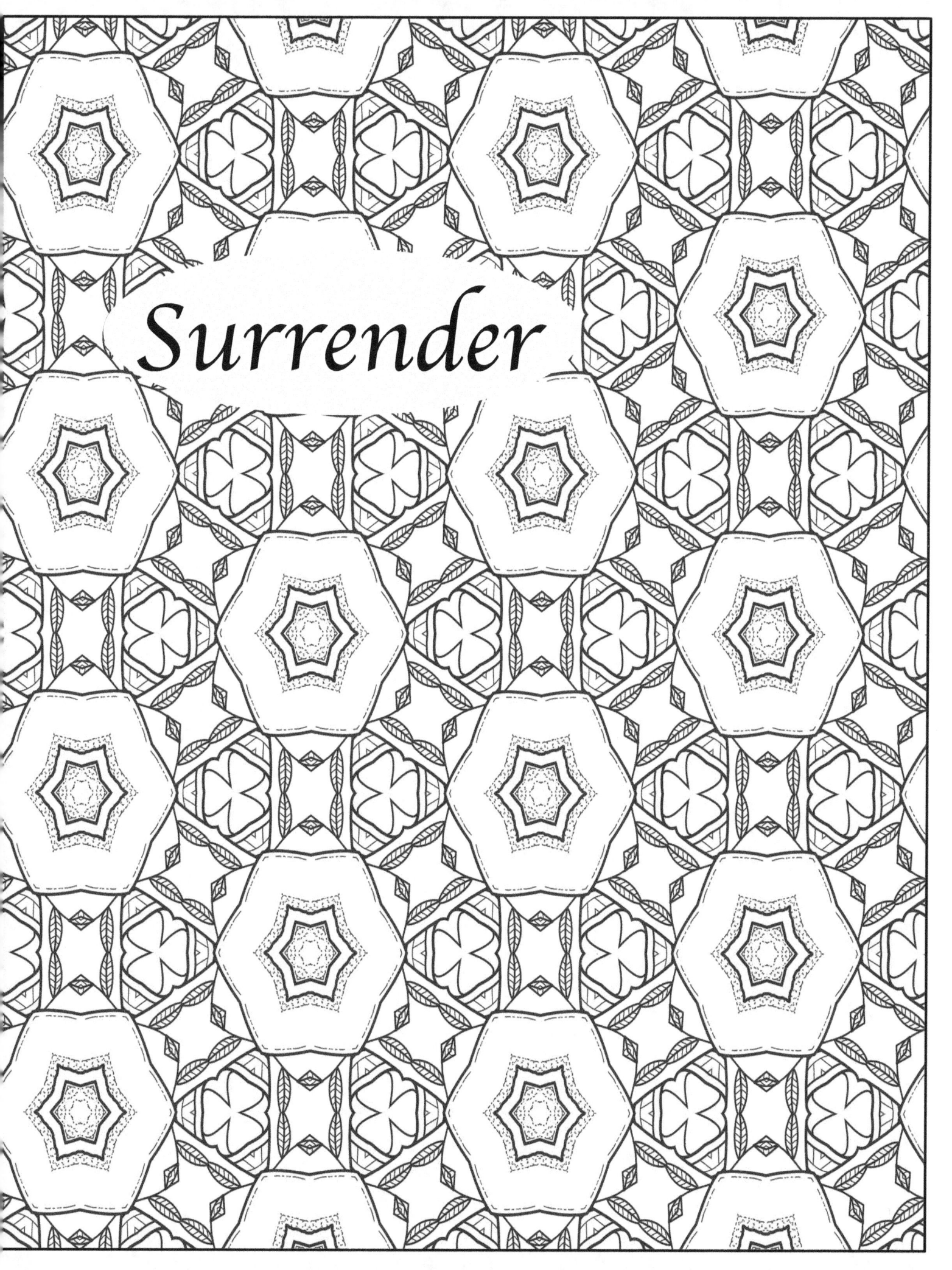

Surrender

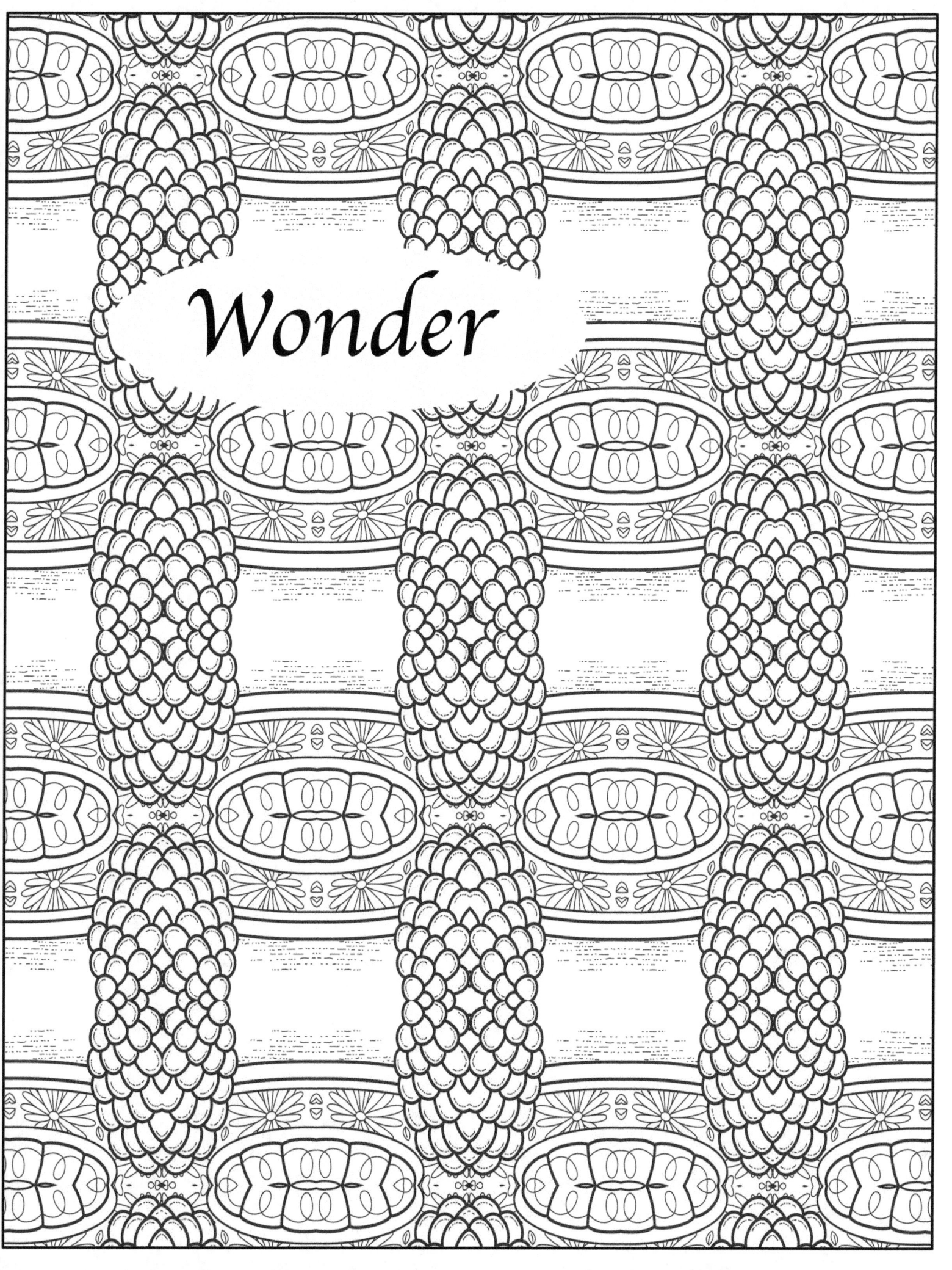

Wonder

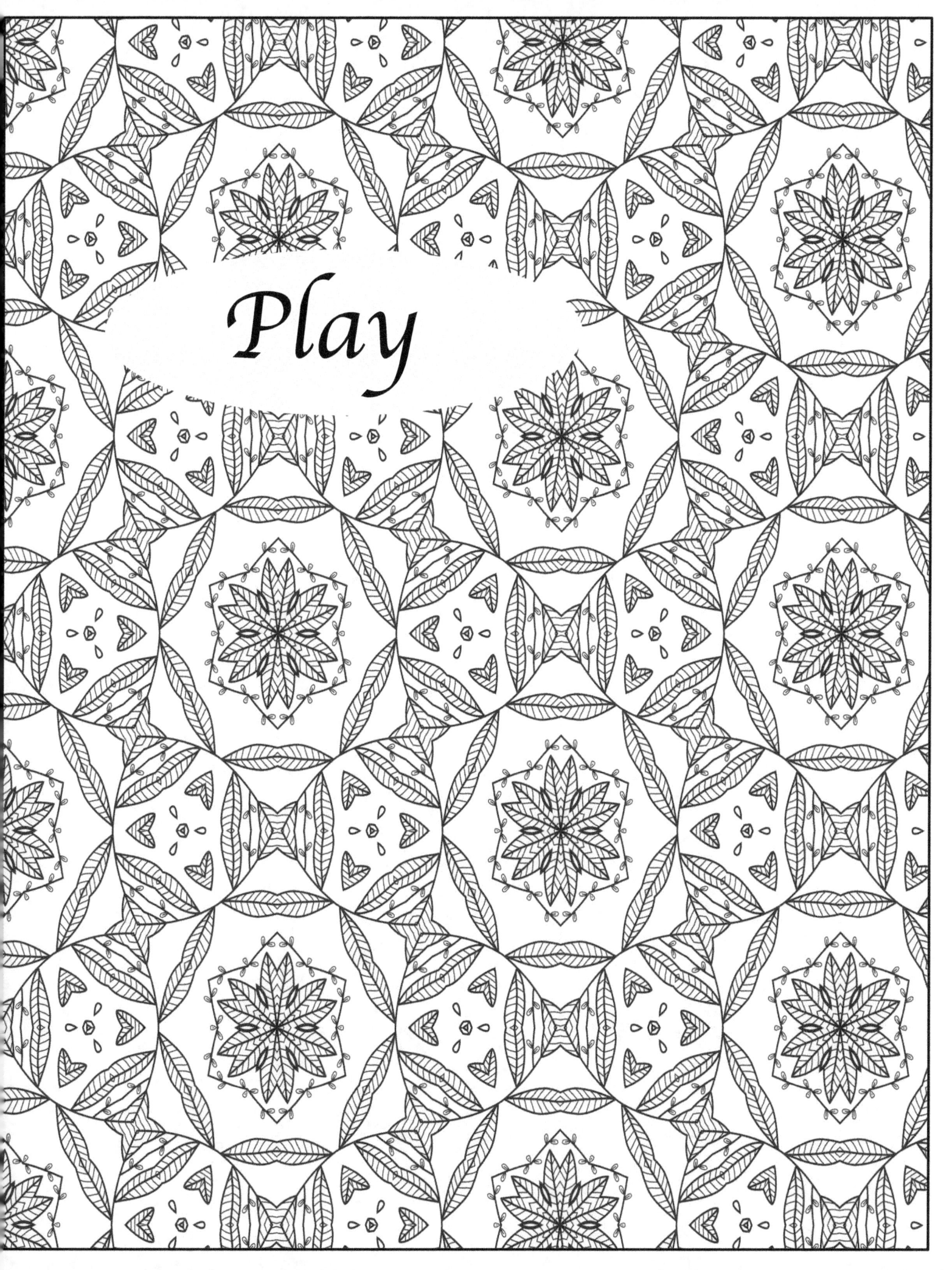

Play

Wish

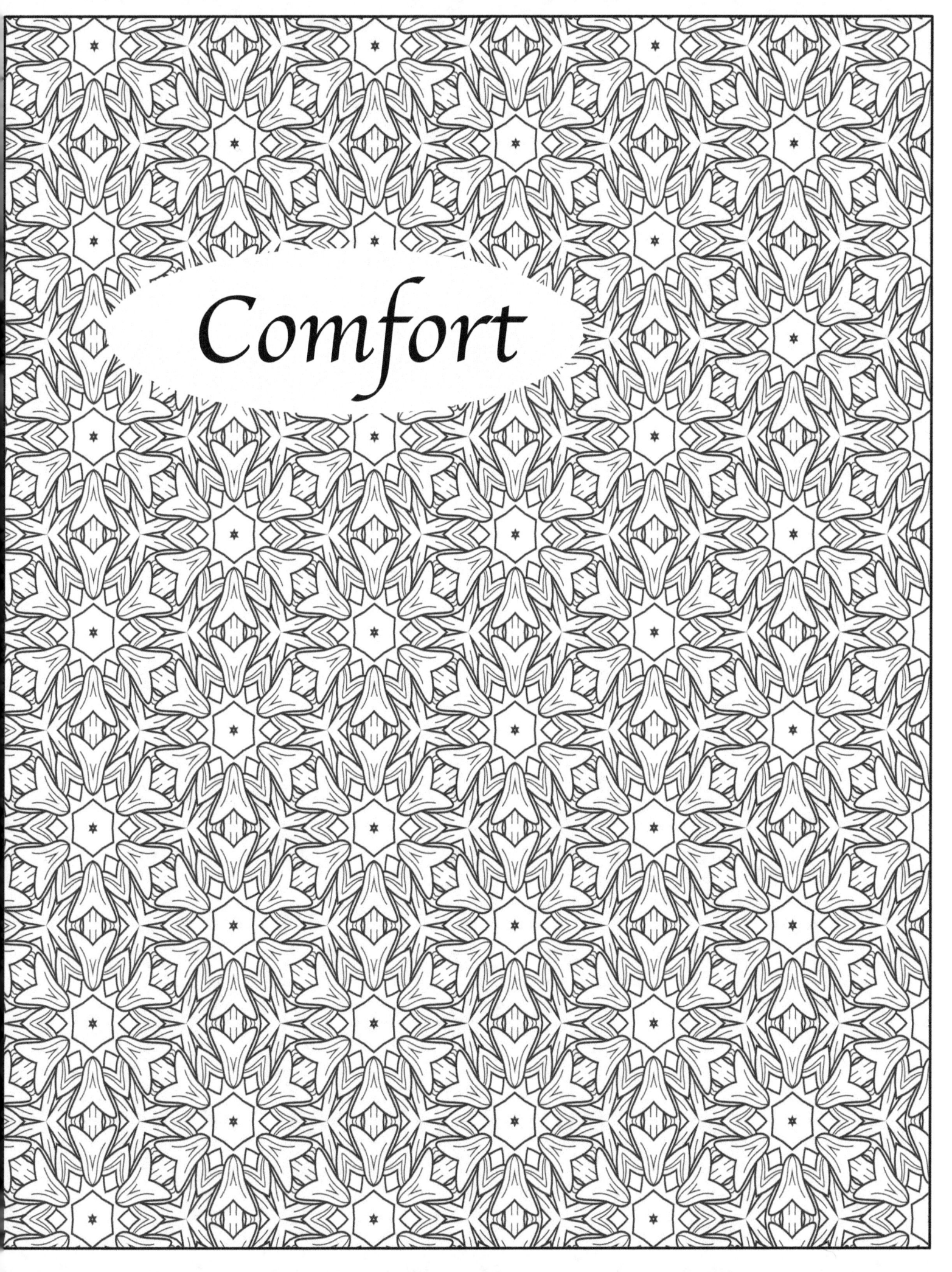

Comfort

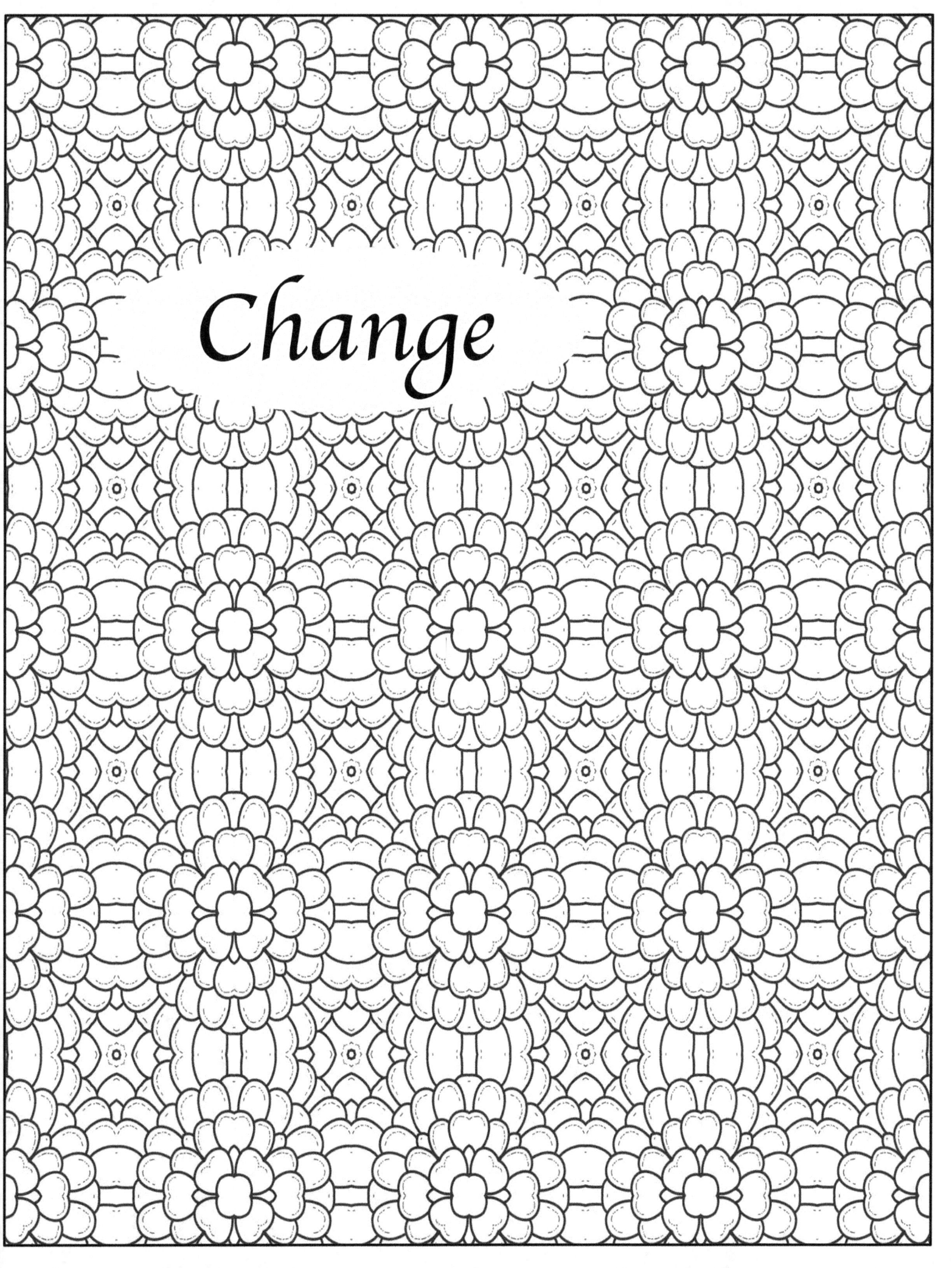

Change

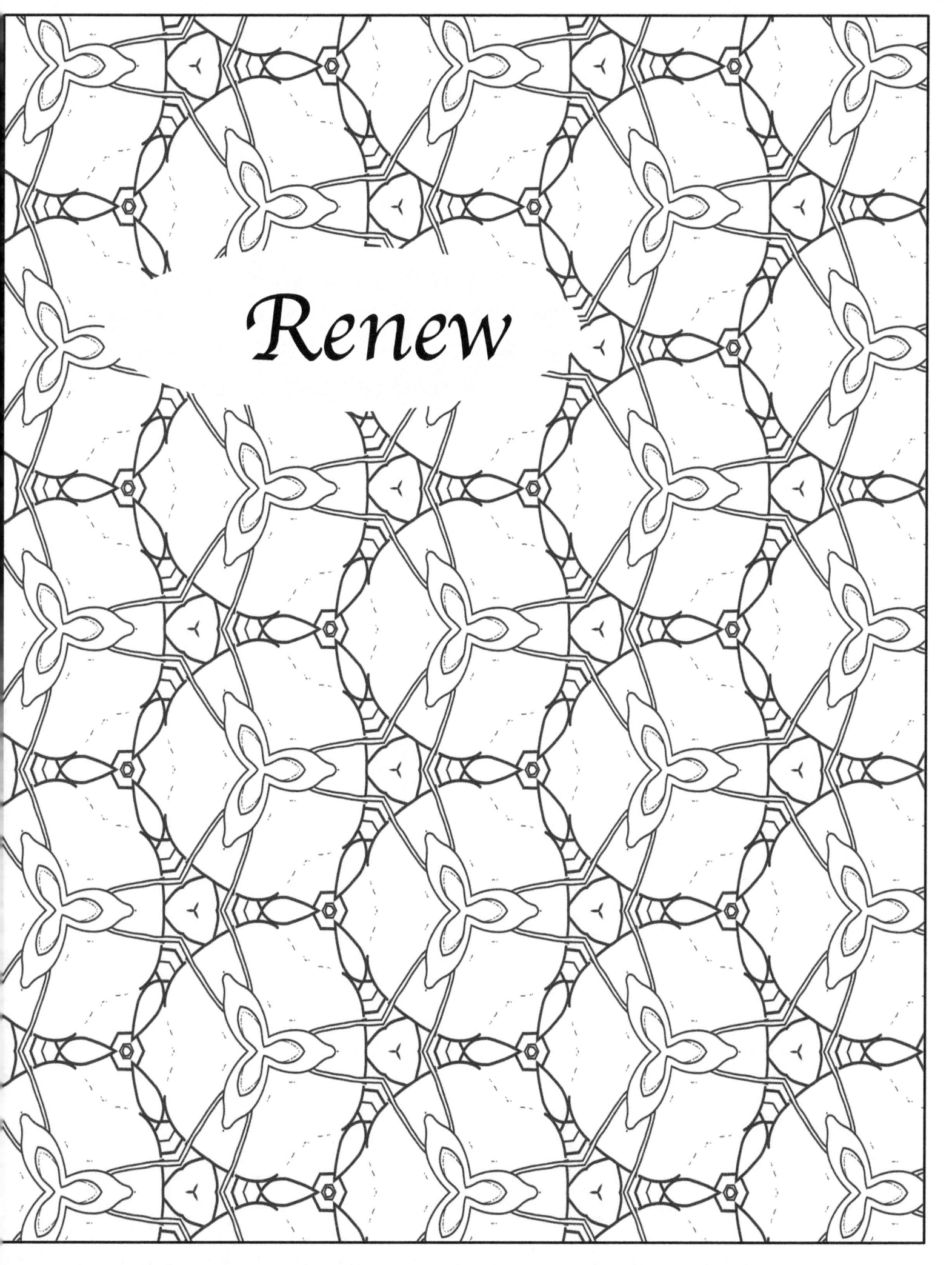

Renew

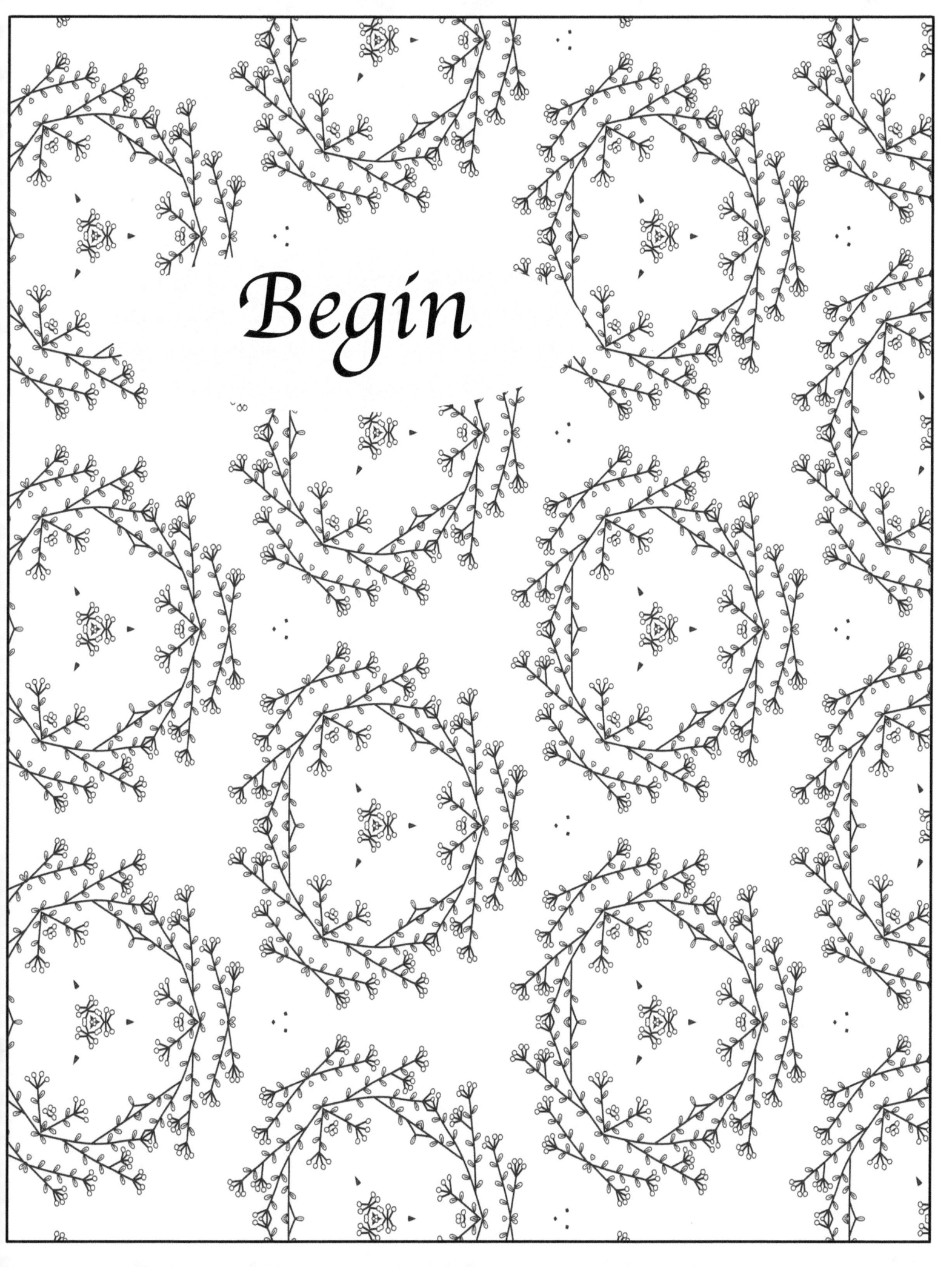

Begin

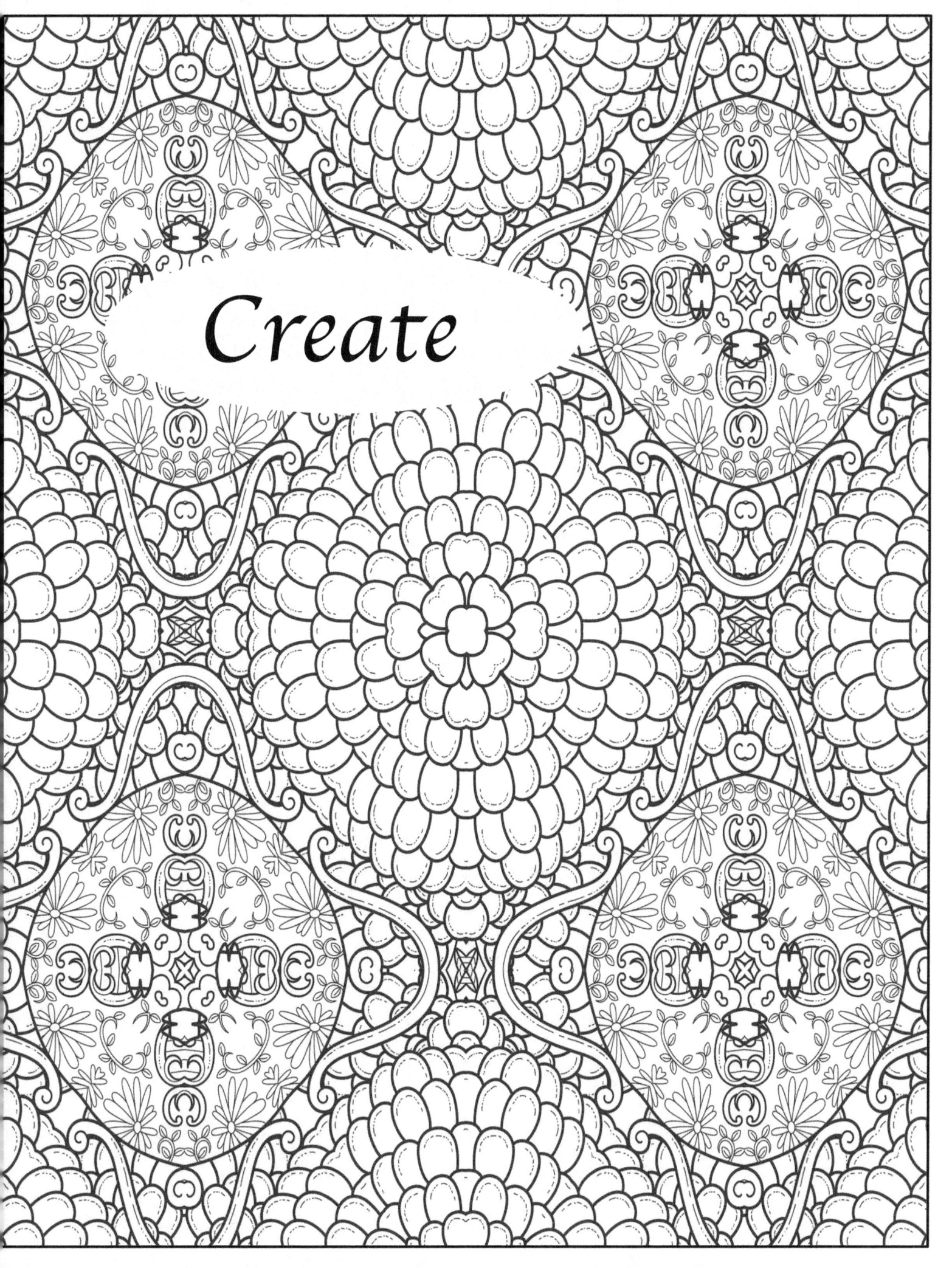

Create

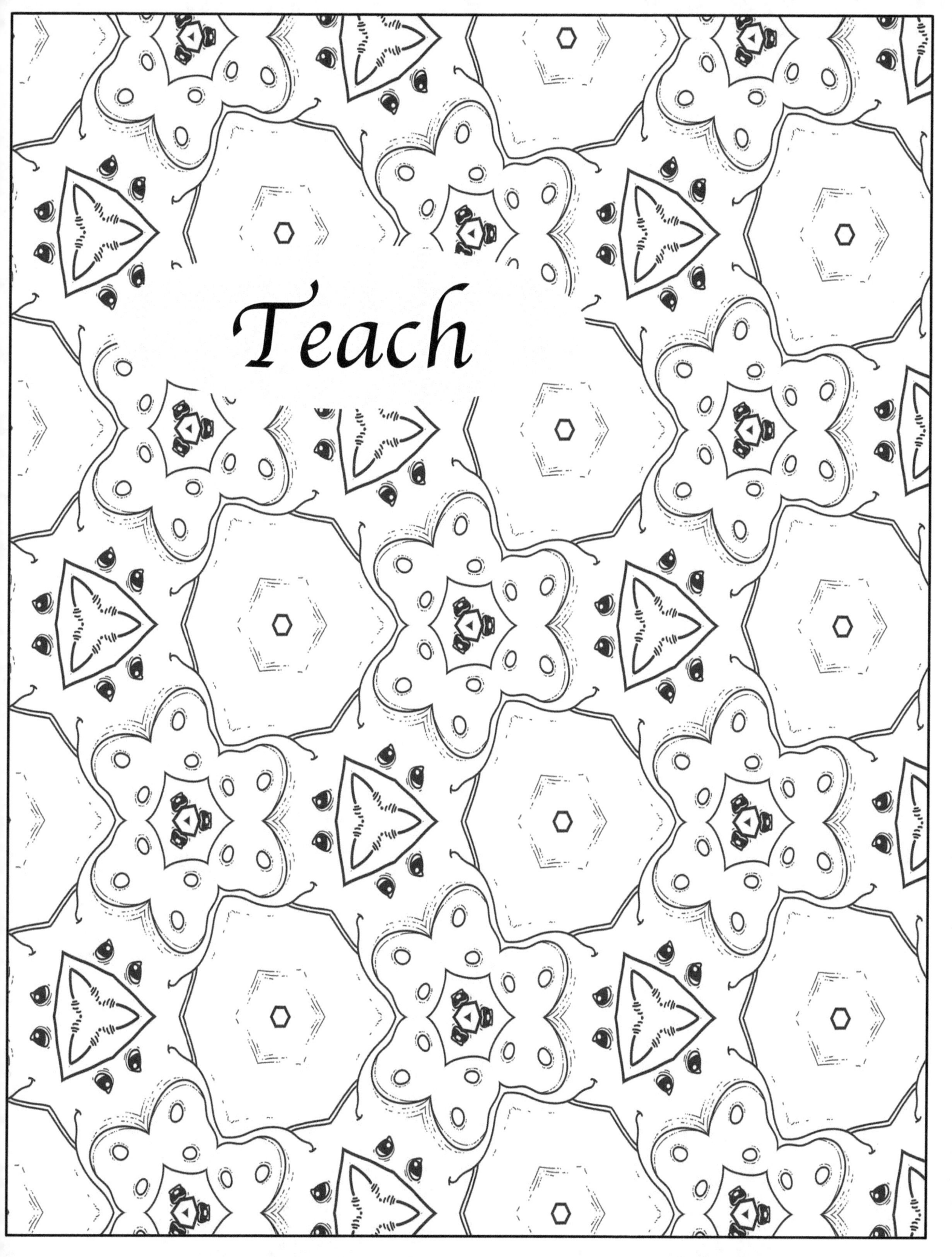

Teach

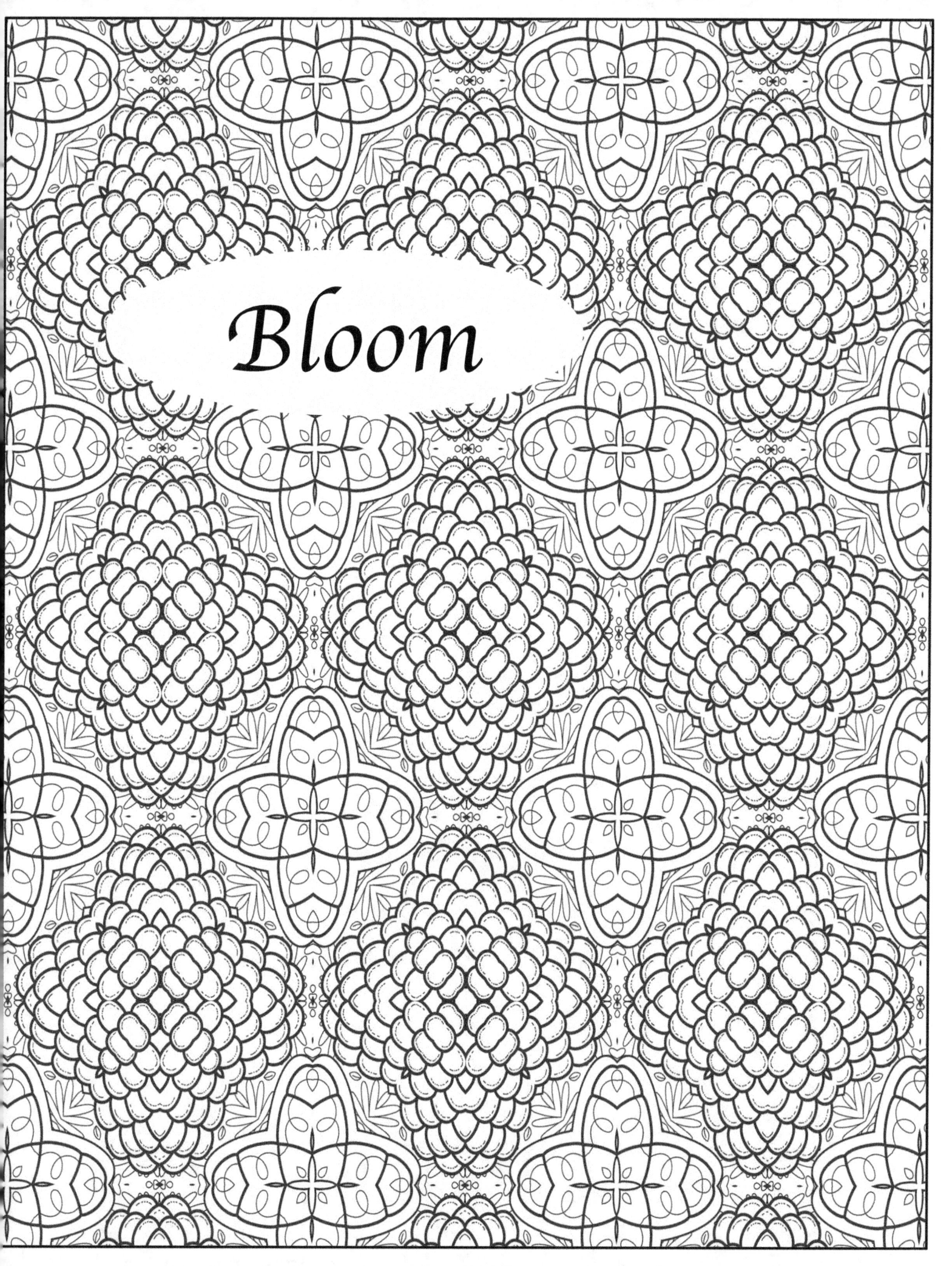

Bloom

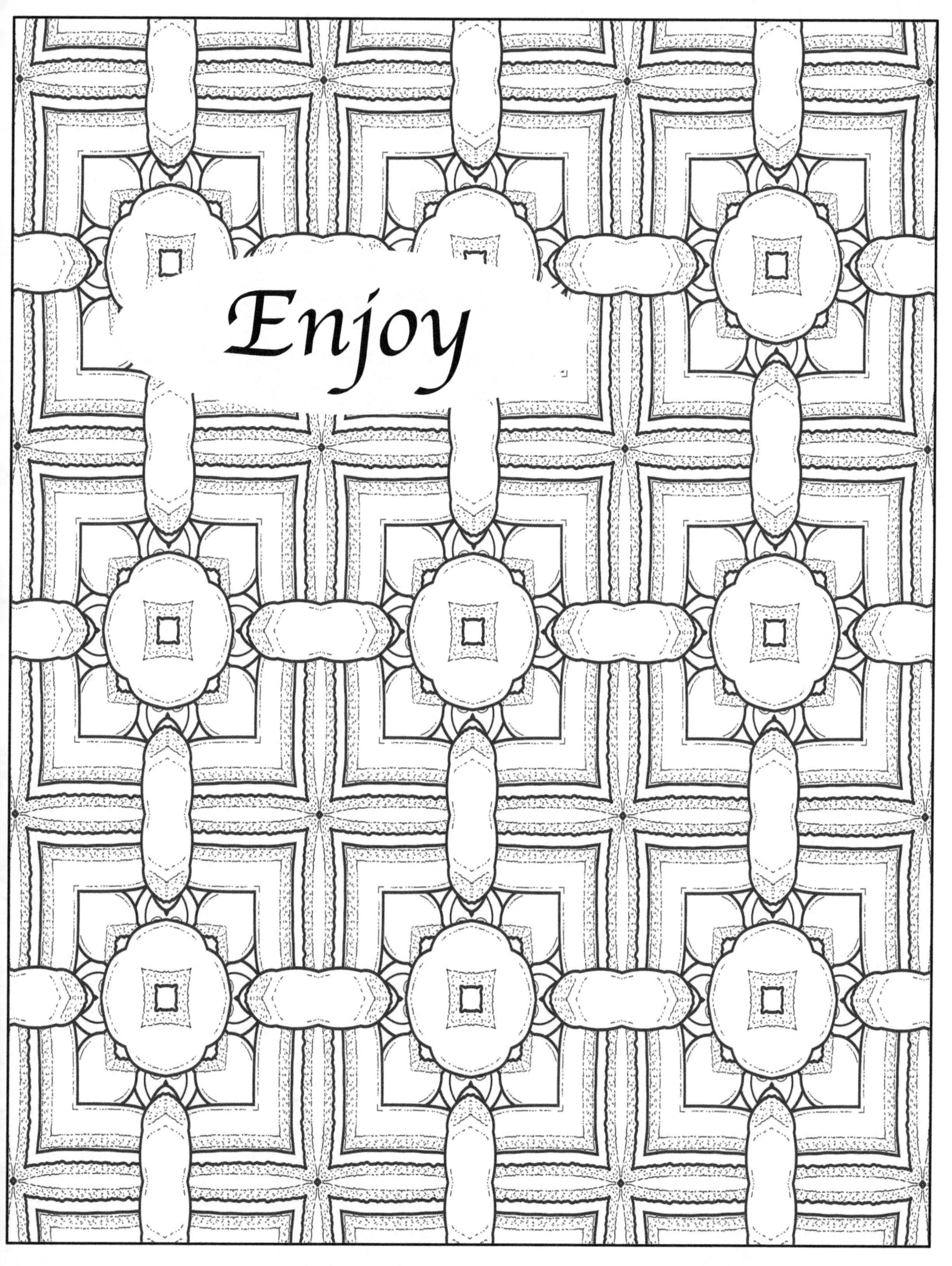